Grandma's Story

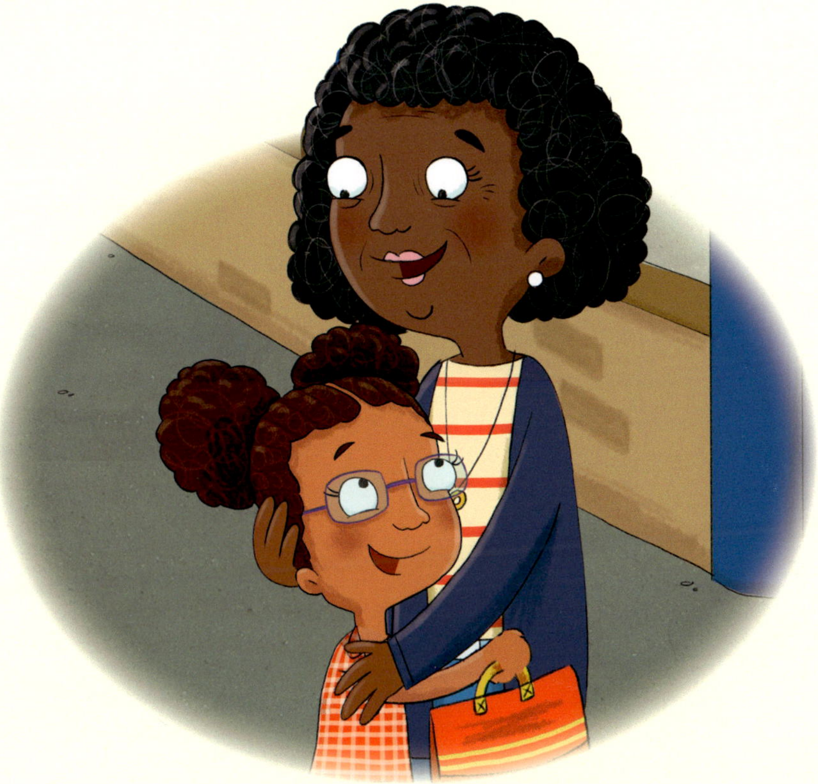

Written by Adam and Charlotte Guillain

RISING STARS

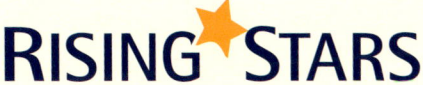

It was the start of a new term at school.

"We're going to learn about what life was like when your grandparents were children!" Mrs Knight told the class. "Please ask your grandparents if they'd like to come in to talk to us."

Asha's insides fluttered with excitement. She was going to her grandma's after school and couldn't wait to ask her.

As soon as Grandma met her in the playground, Asha said, "Please will you come and talk to my class?"

Grandma frowned and shook her head. "I'm not sure," she said. "I get a bit nervous speaking in front of lots of people."

"Oh no, but your stories about when you were little are so good!" Asha said. "Please come!"

Grandma took a deep breath and looked at Asha.

Asha gulped as she waited for her to reply.

"All right, I'll do it!" she said.

Asha jumped up and hugged her.

"I'll ask Mrs Knight to call you," said Asha, skipping along the pavement.

It was arranged for the following Friday.

"That's my grandma," Asha whispered to Tess as her grandma came into the classroom after lunchtime.

Grandma smiled and waved, but Asha saw her hands shaking as she took off her coat. "She looks nervous," Asha thought.

Mrs Knight beamed at the class. "We're very lucky to have Asha's grandma here today to talk to us about life when she was a girl. Welcome!"

Asha's grandma sat down and cleared her throat.

Would you like a glass of water?

Yes please.

Asha watched her grandma take a sip of the drink. Her hands were trembling. Grandma looked around the room and her eyes landed on Asha, who grinned and gave her grandma a big thumbs up.

"Go on, Grandma!" she whispered, her heart thumping.

Grandma took a deep breath. "I-I was b-born in 1960," she stuttered. Grandma coughed and took another gulp of her drink.

Asha bit her lip as the class waited in silence. "You can do it, Grandma," she thought. "Your stories are brilliant!"

Grandma breathed in again. Asha held her breath.

"My family wasn't rich," Grandma continued. "We didn't have many toys or nice things to eat."

Asha kept smiling at her grandma, urging her on.

Grandma caught her eye and gave a little smile back.

"I had two sisters and two brothers," said Grandma. "We lived in a small house so I had to share a bedroom with my sisters. The toilet was outside in the yard so it could be very cold going to the loo!"

"All my clothes were passed on from my sisters," Grandma explained, "but I didn't mind. I loved going to the library every Saturday morning. We'd go to the market and the shops too – there were no supermarkets."

Asha noticed her grandma's hands had stopped shaking.

"Go on, Grandma," she thought again, wondering what story she was going to tell.

"My dad was a bus driver and my mum stayed at home," said Grandma. "It was unusual for women to work then so Mum did the cleaning and cooking in the house. We didn't have dishwashers or washing machines!"

"We didn't have computers either!" she added. "I spent most of my time playing outside in the street with my friends."

Grandma thought for a moment. "We did have a television though. In fact, we were one of the first families in my street to get a colour TV!"

"We got it in the summer of 1969. We thought it was amazing but the screen was actually quite tiny. There were programmes for children but only for one hour a day!"

Asha leaned forward. She hadn't heard this story.

"In July 1969, American astronauts landed on the Moon for the first time. All the neighbours came to our house to watch the first Moon landing on our TV. Our kitchen was full of sandwiches, cakes and jellies, ready for a big tea afterwards."

"I sat on the floor at the front because I was the smallest. We watched in amazement as Neil Armstrong stepped on to the surface of the Moon. Then I needed to go to the toilet!"

Grandma stopped talking, and her hands started to tremble on her knees.

Asha put her hand up. "What happened next?" she asked encouragingly.

Grandma turned to Asha and smiled again. "I was too shy to ask everyone to move, but soon I was desperate. I stood up in front of the television and started to cry!"

"Luckily, my dad lifted me out of the room so I could run out into the yard. When I came back through the kitchen, I saw something move. It was a cat. Then I gasped – it was eating the sandwiches for our tea!"

"Then another cat jumped on the table! I clapped my hands and shouted at the cats. They leaped off the table and jumped out of the window. When I turned around, everyone had come into the kitchen to see what the noise was about."

"Everyone cheered because I'd saved the tea party. All because I'd needed the toilet!"

The class laughed and giggled.

When they'd quietened down, Grandma added, "That night, I couldn't sleep. I remember looking out of my bedroom window at the stars and the Moon."

"My dad tiptoed in, because my sisters were sleeping, and looked at the Moon with me.

"Isn't it amazing to think there are people up there!" I whispered.

"And we've got our very own star down here," he told me.

Grandma smiled.

Mrs Knight began clapping and everyone joined in.

Asha ran over to Grandma and gave her a hug.

"Thank you!" she said. "You were brilliant!"

Grandma beamed at her. "It was fun in the end," she said, "and your smiling face helped! Now, I must dash. I really need the toilet!"

Talk about the story

Answer the questions:

1 Why was Asha's grandma 'not sure' about coming to the school? (page 4)

2 Which day of the week did Asha's grandma visit the school?

3 What year was Asha's grandma born?

4 What does the word 'trembling' mean (page 8)? Can you think of another word to replace it?

5 What job did Asha's grandma's dad do?

6 Why did all the neighbours come to Asha's grandma's house?

7 Have you ever spoken in front of lots of people? Were you nervous? Why? Or why not?

8 Would you like to have been a child in the 1960s? Why? Or why not?

Can you retell the story in your own words?